I0404761

Acknowledgements

Many thanks to Michael Bullis and Ken Kalumuck for their comments on earlier drafts of this guide.

© Jo Anne Schneider 7/2016

Table of Contents

Introduction 1
What is Social Capital? 4
    Connections that lead to resources 5
    Reciprocal, Enforceable Trust 8
    Cultural Cues (cultural capital) 11
Three Different Kinds of Social Capital 15
    Bonding Social Capital 15
    Bridging Social Capital 17
    Linking Social Capital 19
Identifying and Using Social Capital in the Person with Disabilities Networks 21
Organization Social Capital 25
    Social Capital Belonging to the Organization as a Whole 25
    Board Social Capital 28
    Staff Professional Networks 30
Staff Personal Networks 33
Empowering Individuals with Disabilities to Build Social Capital 35
    Building Social Capital to Help Consumers Develop Careers 37
    Building Appropriate Cultural Capital 39
Social Capital and Faith Communities 42
Tips for Effectively Using Social Capital in Employment for People with Disabilities 47
Appendix: The Theory and Research Behind Social Capital ... 51
References 54
Related Publications 57
    In this Series 57
    Other Key Publications by Jo Anne Schneider on Social Capital 57

© **Jo Anne Schneider 7/2016**

© Jo Anne Schneider 7/2016

Introduction

Catherine is an employment specialist at New Day, an agency serving people with developmental disabilities. While attending a networking breakfast sponsored by the local Chamber of Commerce for her agency, Catherine meets Ned, who is the owner of a local pet store. They strike up a conversation and swap cards. Several weeks later, Catherine is trying to find a job for Jacob, who loves animals. She calls Ned to see if Jacob can visit the pet store hoping that her connection with Ned will lead to a job. Ned doesn't return her calls. After several tries, she schedules some time for Jacob to visit the pet store and he has a good visit, talking enthusiastically with Ned and other staff about the animals. Catherine tries to set up another visit, asking if perhaps Jacob could volunteer to learn about working with animals. Ned explains that he really doesn't have time to supervise someone like Jacob and doesn't need any new staff, even though Catherine notes that this store frequently has job openings.

Marjorie also works as an employment specialist for New Day. She is trying to find a job for Caroline, who wants to work with children and dreams of being a day care teacher. Marjorie contacts her friend Jane who is the assistant director of a day care located at a local church and asks if she can bring Caroline over for a visit. Jane talks to her director, who is happy to give Caroline a tour. When they arrive at the church, Caroline breaks into a big smile and says that she went to camp at this church until she graduated from high school two years ago. The day care staff recognize Caroline because the campers did some joint programs with the day care. Caroline has a good visit at the day care and at the end the staff invite her to come again. After several visits,

Marjorie is able to develop a day care assistant job for Caroline at this center. An older teacher who remembers Caroline from her time at camp volunteers to be her mentor to help her learn to work at this day care and perhaps get certified as a day care aid later.

Both of these examples show disability agency staff attempting to use connections to help the individuals they serve find jobs. Through training at their agency, both had learned that social capital, which they thought meant connections, was the key to finding work. Social capital is often touted by experts as important to find work, build social integration, and generally expand the ability of people with disabilities to become part of the community. But Catherine's connections led nowhere while Marjorie was successful. That's because Catherine's connection to Ned really wasn't social capital.

Social capital is widely used in policy, workforce development, human services and by those interested in building community or civic participation. While the concept has a common definition, it is often not defined by those using it, frequently used to mean several different things, and often misunderstood. This guide is designed to explain in practical terms what social capital means and how people involved in employment for people with disabilities can use social capital to help the individuals they work with find and keep jobs. This guide is meant for agency staff, a companion guide is designed for people with disabilities and their families.

The discussion starts by defining social capital and the various ingredients that staff need to pay attention to in identifying and using social capital. Next, the guide uses examples to explore social capital through people with disabilities' network, the networks of disability services organizations, their staff and board. A special section talks about social capital and faith communities because churches, synagogues, mosques, temples

© **Jo Anne Schneider 7/2016**

and other worship communities are often considered natural sources of social capital, but accessing social capital in faith communities can be complicated. A final section summarizes key points in using social capital effectively. While the guide is based on academic research, it does not use academic language or references. Information on the theory behind social capital and key references are in an appendix.

© Jo Anne Schneider 7/2016

What is Social Capital?

Social capital is the social science term for building relationships that help individuals, families and agencies access the resources they need to meet their goals. Social capital is defined as *the social relationships and patterns of reciprocal, enforceable trust that enable people and institutions to gain access to resources like social services, jobs, or government contracts.* Building social capital is a slow process that involves people developing trusting relationships with both other people and organizations. Families and organizations both develop networks of others with similar goals and interests that they exchange information, goods, and services with on a regular basis.

This definition helps us understand why Marjorie was able to use her connections to help Caroline get a job at the day care center while Catherine's connection did not lead anywhere. Social capital is not just a connection you make at a meeting, but comes out of relationships that you have established over time. Both Marjorie and Caroline had established relationships with the day care center. Marjorie had known Jane socially for a number of years and had an established, trusting relationship with her. While Caroline did not have an established relationship with the day care staff, they knew that she was a participant in the camp program that the day care agency had an established relationship with and partnered with in summer programs. As such, they knew that the campers received good social skills training and felt that this training taught similar values to skills needed to work at that day care. At least one of the teachers remembered Caroline well enough to want to be her mentor when she was hired at the day care. Because of these established relationships with Marjorie and Caroline's

© Jo Anne Schneider 7/2016

summer camp, they were willing to give Caroline access to their resources, in this case a job.

While Ned may have enjoyed meeting Catherine at the Chamber of Commerce breakfast and may have known New Day by reputation, he had no established relationship with either Catherine or her agency. He had also not met Jacob before. As such, he had no reason to assume that Jacob would be a good job candidate. While he may have observed Jacob interacting with the animals, he had no personal knowledge of what was involved in employing someone with Jacob's disabilities. Since neither he nor anyone in his networks had hired anyone from New Day, he had no assurances that the individuals they served would work out well as employees or of the kinds of supports that the agency could provide to help Ned succeed. Without any established relationships, or assurances from his broader network of other employers that hiring Jacob could benefit his business, he was unwilling to give him a chance. No established relationship meant no reason to give Jacob access to the jobs at the pet store.

While these examples might imply that agencies should only use the established networks of their staff and the individuals they serve to help them get jobs, social capital is more subtle than that. Taking a look at the ingredients that make up social capital clarifies how it can best be used to help individuals with disabilities find jobs.

Connections that lead to resources

Everyone has connections, but to function as social capital that connection must lead to needed resources. For example, Mark is a person with developmental disabilities that is part of a large, supportive family and an active member in his family's church. His family and friends through church and other networks have

© **Jo Anne Schneider 7/2016**

provided lots of resources for Mark over the years like rides to programs, companions, and even funding for special camps. But this large network did not have the resources to help him find a job. Mark is fascinated with birds of prey and dreamed of working at a park, zoo, or animal rescue organization. His family and friends worked primarily in construction or service sector jobs and knew no-one that had anything to do with birds. As a result, they offered Mark lots of jobs helping out at their companies, but nothing related to his interests.

This does not mean that networks must have connections to a particular job or place to provide social capital. If the networks of either individuals or the agencies that serve them know how to foster necessary connections, that also can generate productive social capital. Mary's experience with education and work offers one example. Mary has cerebral palsy that confines her to a wheelchair, limits her hand movements without assistive technology, and creates challenges speaking clearly. She is very bright and dreamed from a young age of working in scientific computer software design. Her parents, a hospital administrator and real estate agent, had no networks in that field but did know through the organizations they worked with and professional experience how to find the right clubs, college programs and internships to help Mary realize her dreams. Mary participated in computer and science clubs during high school that provided mentoring, internships, and job shadowing at government and private firms needed to make connections that later led to internships during college. Mentors found through these clubs and job experiences guided her to colleges that offered the coursework and connections she needed to develop her career. By her last year in college, Mary had been hired during the summer at a large company where she had interned earlier with the promise of a job after graduation.

© Jo Anne Schneider 7/2016

To serve as social capital for employment, those networks need to have access to paying jobs, not just places that do the kind of work the person with a disability wants to do. For example, Steve wanted to work in disability policy. He had cerebral palsy at a level similar to Mary, with some added learning disabilities, but spoke clearly. Coming from a college educated family, Steve had the support and connections to complete a BA in political science and find internships during college at disability rights organizations. After college, he used these connections to try to find work. But he found that these firms had no money to hire, only providing volunteer and unpaid internship positions. Three years after graduation, he was living on social security and volunteering in a national disability rights organization. While this experience may lead to a job later, at present this rich network cannot provide the employment resources Steve needs.

Networks also need to have access to the right hiring managers, not just organizations with jobs. Take Kira, a young woman on the autism spectrum with real artistic talent served by a large, established disability services organization Disability Workforce Services. Kira wanted to help design displays in a store and her job developer, Grace had heard through a training that she should try to create a customized job for her clients based on their skills and interests. Customized jobs involve identifying an individual's interests and skills, then finding a work place that needs someone to do a task that fits those skills and interests. Often these jobs are not regular jobs advertised by the company but are specially created for the person with a disability.

Disability Workforce Services had strong connections to a number of national and regional grocery and big box chains, usually placing their clients as baggers, shelvers or cleaning staff.

© **Jo Anne Schneider 7/2016**

Grace had learned the theory of customized employment, but not how to identify places likely to create a customized job or set one up. Grace told Kira that they should look for display design jobs at Walmart and similar places where her organization had connections. But Grace had no idea how to find out who hired people to help with this kind of design work or even how decisions about displays were made. As a result, her connections were no help in finding Kira the kind of job she wanted.

This examples highlight that in order to identify effective social capital, staff need to ask not simply if the individual with a disability and their networks, or the disability employment agency's networks, have connections, but if they have the right connections to find a paying job doing the kind of work the person with a disability wants to do. If not, other mechanisms can be used to build social capital or provide links to resources that will help the person with a disability develop appropriate social capital over time. Ways to do this will be discussed later in this guide.

Reciprocal, Enforceable Trust

Why would someone use their connections to help someone find a job? The answer is a sense of trust and mutual obligation. The kind of trust that leads to social capital is not generalized trust like trusting your neighbors, the police, or the local government. Its specific trust in an individual, their networks, or the organizations they are associated with. Usually, to effectively generate social capital, those helping someone find a job and the person or organization hiring has an established, reciprocal relationship with each other. The relationship can also be between the person or organization doing the hiring and the person with the disability.

For example, compare the kinds of trust involved in the hiring decisions for Caroline and Jacob. Ned, the pet store owner, was not interested in even giving Jacob a chance to volunteer because he did not have an established, trusting relationship with New Day or Catherine, Jacob's employment specialist. Ned did know that New Day had a good reputation in the community and was a member of the chamber, but that generated only enough generalized trust to allow Ned to consent to have Jacob visit once. On the other hand, Caroline benefited from the reciprocal trust between her employment specialist Marjorie and her friend Jane who worked for the day care and the established relationship between Caroline's camp and the day care, both hosted by the same church. Jane and Marjorie had helped each other out for years and Jane's director trusted Jane's judgment that Marjorie would not present Caroline as a potential employee if she didn't know she had the skills and attitude to work out. The same was true for Mary, who developed trusting relationships with her potential employer over time initially through contacts at college and then internships at that agency.

Trusting relationships can come from organizations, not just individuals. For example, one reason the day care gave Caroline a chance was that they knew and trusted the camp she had attended during school. Likewise, Mary's initial connections came through her college computer and science clubs, then her college.

Those organization relationships don't necessarily need to be through people or organizations directly known to each other. Catherine found another pet shop that eventually hired Jacob to help care for animals. The manager of this shop shared with

Catherine that she agreed to give Jacob a trial job because she had learned that New Day was a subsidiary of the local Arc and this manager's sister had hired people through the Arc in another state successfully for years. The established reputation of the Arc as a trusted employment provider based on real world experience, even from another location, swayed her decision.

Established, reciprocal relationships are important because they mean that a relationship will not be damaged based on one bad experience. Agencies like New Day and Disability Workforce Services depend on their established reputations to successfully do their work. For example, Disability Workforce Services has placed people with significant mental illness and developmental disabilities in entry level cleaning, shelving and support positions in chain stores for years. While these companies know that the agency does a good job of screening their program participants and giving them soft skill training before referring them for jobs, they also know that one in five hires does not work out. They continue to use this agency as an employment service because they know that most of their participants remain on the job and perform successfully and that if someone doesn't work out, they will be quickly replaced. It is these established relationships with employers that keep employers hiring from the agency and families of people with disabilities using this organization, even when the jobs found for people with disabilities may not be what the people with disabilities want.

This suggests that identifying networks that can effectively find jobs means looking at the strength of the relationships as well as the number and simple availability of connections. Identifying relationships should involve looking both for relationships between organizations that the person with disabilities and their networks are affiliated with as well as individual networks. The

© Jo Anne Schneider 7/2016

disability services agency's own trusted networks are a key resource for employment for the individuals it serves.

Cultural Cues (cultural capital)

People use their social capital to help those that they think will represent them well and help them preserve established relationships. This final ingredient in effectively using social capital involves knowing the right ways to behave, speak, dress, etc. to encourage others to help the person with a disability find work or employ them in their company. In social science definitions of social capital, the ability to fit in is called *norms, cultural capital, or cultural cues.* Appropriate cultural cues differ depending on the network, workplace, community, and other factors. Cultural capital is separate from social capital, but it is essential for activating social capital. Besides looking for networks, staff and people with disabilities need to understand the important cultural cues that will enable social capital to be effective.

Cultural capital appears as an important factor in the successful employment stories described earlier. The day care hired Caroline, in part, because they knew that the values she had learned at camp were similar to those practiced at the day care. Equally important, the organization assigned a staff member who knew her as her mentor to help her learn the job, including the all important culture of the workplace. Mary learned how to interact with computer software designers and use the right jargon through her high school clubs and college experiences. While Steve is still volunteering, he has learned the cultural cues needed to work in a disability advocacy agency through his internship experiences.

© Jo Anne Schneider 7/2016

Problems with cultural capital can take many forms. In some cases, it is a problem with the way a person presents themselves or the case for employment. For example, Kira, the young artist, had been placed twice by her agency before they started looking for a customized job for her. The first job as a shelver in a big box store ended in two weeks because Kira felt that she was treated badly on the job. While some of this was Kira's sensitivities, her employers reported that they found Kira's clothing and mannerisms "odd." Kira quit a 2nd job in a warehouse because it didn't fit her interests and she felt she didn't fit in.

Staff with limited work or life experience also may be missing the cultural cues to effectively find jobs for the people they serve. Grace, her employment specialist, had no idea what was involved with doing the kind of store displays Kira wanted to do and was at a loss to help her find an appropriate job because she lacked the cultural information on how one became involved in doing marketing displays. Catherine, Jacob's employment specialist, told Ned all about how it was important for self-esteem, skills development, and social integration for Jacob to work in the community, but had not learned what the pet shop needed to run efficiently and did not present the business case for hiring a person with a disability.

The good news about cultural capital is that it can be learned. Everyone who successfully moves through life learns to fit into a number of different cultural environments. Most of us learn that we dress, behave, and talk differently in different places. For example, talking and dressing one way with friends and another at a workplace or church. Sometimes this is as simple as helping someone like Kira learn how to dress and act appropriately for a specific job. Learning how to identify tasks a

© Jo Anne Schneider 7/2016

business might need but may not advertise as a job can also be taught through trainings and experience.

At other times, this can be complicated. For example, the worlds of marketing design, policy, software design, and wild birds require specialized training, knowledge, and have their own unique cultures. It is difficult for a general staff like employment specialists or job developers to learn this culture, especially with participants with diverse interests. As discussed below, it may be better to identify mentors or people within the person with disability's networks with this knowledge to help them learn the appropriate cultural cues.

In some cases, cultural capital issues are difficult to break through. For example, Mark, the young man who wanted to work with birds of prey, had family and church networks that were supportive of people with developmental disabilities but had deeply ingrained cultural beliefs that someone like Mark could probably do cleaning and lifting, but not much else. When his employment specialist sought to connect him with a wildlife rescue organization and pursue interviews with staff at a state park, his family complained that the agency should instead just "find him a job." Successfully placing Mark involved convincing his family that this slower approach to job placement was worthwhile.

In other cases, culture is ingrained in hiring practices. Take for example Selma, a blind woman with a graduate degree in human resources and significant experience in providing professional development and trainings on working with people with disabilities. Selma's vocational rehabilitation counselor learned of a staff training job in a related government agency where she had many contacts. Selma had all the skills and the appropriate

© Jo Anne Schneider 7/2016

cultural knowledge to do this job well, but she could not meet one hiring criteria in the job description. This agency only hired from within, with an agency culture that people started as vocational rehabilitation specialists and worked their way up to other positions in the agency. The job required that the training specialist have worked as a vocational rehabilitation counselor for 7 years and had managed vocational rehabilitation counselors for 3 years. This requirement was unrelated to any of the actual skills required in the job description and was just meant to keep those who had not come up through the ranks in this agency or a similar one from being hired. Even though she understood the culture of the agency, she could not successfully compete for the position because of this agency requirement. Changing this situation would probably require civil rights complaints against the agency and would be difficult to enforce even if they were successful.

This discussion of the role of cultural capital in effectively using social capital implies that staff need to pay attention both to the nature of the networks and the cultural cues that both they and the individuals they serve need to display in order to convince a connection to facilitate employment. In some cases, this involves simply paying attention and using the right cultural cues. In other cases, appropriate culture needs to be learned by staff or the person with the disability, or both. In other cases, successfully finding someone a job involves bringing in someone else who is part of a network one is trying to access who can teach appropriate cultural capital and use the cultural cues needed to gain entry to a company or network of those with needed resources.

© **Jo Anne Schneider 7/2016**

Three Different Kinds of Social Capital

Social capital researchers identify three types of social capital, bonding, bridging and linking. Bonding social capital involves long established networks of close friends, family, or professional networks of people who are similar and share the same values. Bridging social capital means networks that cross boundaries of culture, region, or some other significant difference, but where everyone in the network are generally equal. Linking social capital involves reciprocal, enforceable trust across power boundaries like an employer and their staff person or an agency and the government entity that funds it. While each kind of social capital works differently, each is equally important in the quest to help people with disabilities find the resources they need to find jobs or fulfill other life goals.

Bonding Social Capital

Bonding social capital networks often involve the people you trust most and can rely on no matter what. For example, friends, family, or the people in a faith community where you have attended for years. These are the people and organizations that both individuals and staff turn to first when seeking any resource because they are most likely to try to help. For example, family and close friends are more likely to use their networks to help a person with a disability find jobs. For this reason, trainings for discovery, the first step in developing customized jobs, ask staff to identify the people in an individual's personal networks. As discussed below, discovery involves both identifying a person with a disability's interests and skills and the connections available to help find work.

© **Jo Anne Schneider 7/2016**

Bonding networks can also be professional or personal networks outside of family and friends. For example, the disability agency that wrote the job description only hiring from within that agency or similar ones was practicing bonding social capital by making it difficult for outsiders to get hired. Disability agency staff in a community can form bonding networks where they share job openings and insights on how to serve their program participants better. Hobbies like model railroading, dog breeding, or bird watching can develop bonding networks. Or they can include people from a particular religion, ethnic or religious group.

The important thing about bonding social capital is that people share the same culture and that it is difficult for outsiders to get in or use the network's resources. Bonding networks are often safe, for example, an agency where the individuals served and staff become comfortable with each other and individuals with disabilities are hired for jobs at the agency that they would have difficulty finding outside. But this safe environment is a closed environment, and means that the individual is not integrated into the community.

Bonding networks may offer limited resources because of the closed nature of the network. For example, Mark's network had lots of resources to find him a job cleaning, shelving or providing other physical labor, but nothing to help him find work that met his interests. Given that everyone in the network worked in blue collar or service sector jobs, the culture of the network did not support trying something different. In order to help Mark meet his goals, he would need to look outside these networks.

Bonding networks can either be a supportive environment that will help people succeed or have limited vision of people's

© **Jo Anne Schneider 7/2016**

capabilities. For example, Kira's bonding network of family and church community recognized and honored her artistic talent, but many in that network thought her mannerisms and social awkwardness meant that she was not employable. People in this network either commented that they couldn't help her find work, or suggested she work doing some form of manual labor that did not involve interacting with people. As such, that network needed to be used carefully in helping her find appropriate work.

Bonding networks are important resources for employment development, but they may have their limits. While it is important to identify social capital resources in these networks both for people with disabilities and within staff and agency networks, they may not be sufficient. Identifying and developing bridging and linking social capital is equally important for people with disabilities and the people that aid them.

Bridging Social Capital

Bridging social capital involves reciprocal, trusting relationships developed across group boundaries. For example, Mary, the young woman starting a career in scientific software design had established networks of family and friends with no knowledge of this profession, but she developed connections to others in her chosen profession first through youth involved in after school clubs in high school, then among classmates and through her internships in college. To become part of the world of software designers, she needed to learn their language, appropriate ways to talk and interact with others as well as computer skills. As she develops professional relationships in this network of computer professionals over time, she is likely to both benefit from their

© **Jo Anne Schneider 7/2016**

connections to find jobs and progress in her career, as well as provide information to others in that network. These networks involve different people and different cultural capital from the middle class people in her family's social networks, but otherwise they are equals.

As with Catherine's experience with Ned, the pet store owner she met at Chamber of Commerce breakfast, bridging social capital does not develop over a one time connection between people with no other social capital connections. The two people need to develop a basis for trust and reciprocity first. However, if Catherine continued to get to know Ned and served with him on a Chamber committee, this relationship might develop into bridging social capital. Likewise, bridging social capital could be activated for a new employee, individual served by an agency, or club member by using the social capital of the organization. For example, Catherine was able to place Jacob at another pet store based on a social capital connection of her parent organization, the Arc, with someone in the pet store manager's personal bonding networks. Mary got her first internship because of her high school club's relationship with that employer. Her college internship coordinator found the internship that led to a job through a relationship with that company.

These examples highlight two important aspects of bridging social capital. First, bridging connections usually come through a bridging individual or joining an organization related to the network the person wants to join. In Mary's case, joining the high school computer club gave her entry into the social capital resources affiliated with that club. The college internship coordinator served as a bridging individual to help her gain entry to other employers.

© **Jo Anne Schneider 7/2016**

Second, using bridging social capital involves learning the cultural capital important in the new network. Particularly in the male dominated world of software designers, Mary's high school club staff and college internship coordinator would not have referred her if they felt she had not learned the appropriate social skills to succeed. Caroline was offered a job at the day care center because she had learned appropriate social skills for this workplace at her camp and demonstrated them when she visited.

As with cultural capital, bridging social capital can be built for individuals, staff, and organizations. Ways to build social capital will be discussed below. It is important to remember that the goal is to develop lasting reciprocal relationships across boundaries. This involves both developing connections and learning the appropriate cultural cues to interact appropriately in the new network.

Linking Social Capital

Like bridging social capital, linking social capital involves crossing boundaries, but the person or organization receiving support from the network usually has less power than the one providing the connection. For example, an established professional serving as a mentor for a person with a disability who wants to enter that profession or a government agency contract manager and a disability services agency. We can see many examples of linking social capital in the examples in this guide. The internship coordinators and high school club staff who helped Mary were all linking social capital connections. Likewise, the day care teacher who chose to mentor Caroline was a linking resource.

© Jo Anne Schneider 7/2016

While the person receiving advice and links to jobs is in an unequal relationship to the person providing social capital access, linking social capital is still a reciprocal relationship. Mary, Caroline, and others that receive internships or successful job leads provide benefits to that profession and organization through their quality work. The same is true of the relationship between a funder and an organization providing service. The government entity or funder fulfills its mission through the goods and services offered by its successful contractors.

The recipients of linking social capital also contribute to the network by referring other good candidates or organizations that can provide services needed by government or a private organization. Once established in their careers, they help build and expand the network by serving as linking social capital to others. These actions also develop reciprocal, enforceable trust within the linking network.

As with bridging social capital, successfully using linking social capital involves using the appropriate cultural cues expected by the linking network. No-one is going to refer someone for a job or internship if they don't dress appropriately, know the basic language of the profession and otherwise look like they will fit in. However, if someone lacks some of the social skills but comes through an established individual or organization, a linking social capital connection may provide the tips on appropriate cultural capital to help the newcomer become a successful employee and member of the network.

© Jo Anne Schneider 7/2016

Identifying and Using Social Capital in the Person with Disabilities Networks

Job development has always involved making connections for the person looking for a job. Family and friends have often used their social capital to help people with disabilities find work. For example, I once had a skilled tradesman who was deaf work in my home. He shared that he had learned his trade from his father and was working in the same company. On multiple occasions, family members use their connections to find work for a person with a disability. For example, David works in a small accountant's office filing, copying, and doing other clerical tasks and has worked there full time for over 10 years. His parents knew the firm owners socially and used their bonding social capital to find work for David. David received no employment help from an agency or voc rehab.

In my earlier work with low income job seekers, in study after study, more than half found their jobs through personal networks. Personal networks also play a prominent role in finding people with disabilities work. For this reason, employment specialists, job developers and other disability services agency staff involved in helping people with disabilities find work are encouraged to identify personal networks for the people they serve and them to help with locating jobs.

Staff can identify networks in several ways. In some cases, agencies encourage staff to create a support team for the individual that includes relevant family and friends. This team could either provide contacts for work or use their own networks to identify people who can help. In other cases, staff ask people with disabilities and their families or other significant supporters to identify people in their network with the

© Jo Anne Schneider 7/2016

expectation they can help. This often consists of asking individuals and their families to name the people in their network, list their relationship to the person with a disability, and list ways they help the person out or could help in the future.

This technique is used often in discovery, the first stage of developing jobs related to a person's interests and skills. Staff interview the person with a disability and their family, often in the individual's home to learn about their gifts, skills, limitations and interests. Close family and friends are also interviewed. In the process, lists of individuals they know that have some connection to those interests are identified, with the expectation they can help find a job in that field or help identify a place to create a customized job.

However, simply listing connections is not identifying social capital. Remember that social capital networks have access to needed resources and are willing to put those connections to work for the person with the disability. Simply identifying someone in the person's personal network in that field might not meet these criteria. For example, Steve and his family were active as advocates for people with disabilities, which should have meant that he had many connections that could help him find a job in his field. However, that network consisted of underfunded agencies that could provide volunteer work but not paid work. Kira's network included many people who worked in stores of all kinds, but the people with those connections did not believe that she had the social skills and work ethic to successfully find a job so they were unwilling to help her. While Mark's social and church networks did not include anyone who worked with wild birds, a relative did work as a grounds keeper in a wild life refuge. But this person had no

© Jo Anne Schneider 7/2016

connections to the skilled professionals that worked directly with birds.

For this reason, identifying networks needs to involve asking three questions:

1. Does anyone in the individual's personal networks either work in the field where s/he has an interest or work in a place that is related to that interest?
2. Does that person have useful connections to places or people that could lead to a paying job related to that interest?
3. Is that person willing to use those connections to help the person with a disability find work in that field?

These questions need to be answered for anyone identified as part of the individual with a disability's social network. If the answer is yes, staff should proceed by interviewing the person with appropriate network connections both about the work and the kind of cultural capital needed to function in that field. Asking the network connection to mentor the person with disabilities to help them learn the cultural cues and behavior they will need to succeed would be the next step. Mentors can serve as the bridging link into that network as well as help identify ways interests can translate into a viable job.

If those contacts don't exist, staff can use a number of mechanisms to build links into target networks. Staff can build bridging social capital for the people with disabilities they serve through several mechanisms. Identifying clubs, professional organizations, or venues to participate in activities related to the interest with others with similar interests is one key strategy. For example, Mark could develop both the cultural capital and connections to get a job working with birds of prey by joining a local club for people interested in bird rescue. Kira could enroll in a marketing design course at a local community college. Sometimes, people can join virtual clubs of others with mutual interests, then meet them in person for joint activities around the interest. This can lead to developing bridging relationships. In both cases, staff would need to work with them to ensure that they both develop productive connections with other members of these groups and develop appropriate cultural capital.

© **Jo Anne Schneider 7/2016**

Organization Social Capital

Organizations have social capital in their own right, as organizations. Organizational social capital is more than just the sum total of the social capital of its staff and board, but comes from the relationships the organization has established over time. For example, Disability Workforce Services has a network of employers that it has developed over time which new staff can access to find jobs for the people they serve. Organizations also have networks of funders, government agencies, and other organizations that support their work that can also be put to work to help find jobs for their participants. This chapter looks carefully at the ways that both organizational social capital and the social capital of the people affiliated with the organization can be used to help people with disabilities find jobs.

Social Capital Belonging to the Organization as a Whole

Organizational social capital comes from two places: 1) the established reputation of the organization and 2) social capital through relationships with other organizations that the agency has developed over time. Take the way that Marjorie was able to use the Arc's reputation to find a job for Jacob. The pet store hired Jacob because they believed that Arcs were a good source for employees with disabilities. This name brand's reputation made the difference in hiring decisions. The same can be true for any organization that is visible in a community over time. An organization can foster this kind of social capital by participating actively in community events or organizations like the Chamber of Commerce or service organizations like Rotary.

Partnerships to provide services can also create these kinds of social capital networks. For example, regularly developed

© Jo Anne Schneider 7/2016

volunteer activities like social activities in nursing homes, volunteering in soup kitchens, or fostering boy and girl scout troops that include people with disabilities and encourage adults with disabilities at the agency to serve as assistant scoutmasters can build these relationships. In cases like a soup kitchen, Habitat for Humanity or other organizations that draw volunteers from many organizations, this can build relationships with both the organization offering the service and the churches, scout troops, or other organizations that are also sources of volunteers.

These organizations not only provide potential places that individuals with disabilities can find work, their staff and participants can serve as bridging or linking connections for people with disabilities. For instance, a scout master may work as an HR representative in an agency looking for someone to serve as a facilitator and advocate for people with disabilities in a large company. If Steve was connected to this scout master, she may be able to help him find a job. The head of volunteers at a soup kitchen might reveal that the volunteer liaison for a church that provides meals at a homeless shelter where the disability agency also sends volunteers regularly is the falcon expert at a bird sanctuary, providing an important connection for Mark.

An often overlooked organizational social capital network for disability services agencies is their suppliers, organizations providing professional services, and their sponsors or funders. Accounting firms, IT service companies, web designers, printers, food and office supply companies, clinics providing medical services, payroll or billing services, have established relationships that can be used as networks for people served by the agency. Likewise, foundations and government agencies

© **Jo Anne Schneider 7/2016**

funding programs have a vested interest in their success. Agency staff could turn to these organizations to provide internships or contacts into other networks that fit the interests of people with disabilities served by the agency.

Effectively using organizational networks from suppliers and other professional networks belonging to the organization involves both educating those suppliers about people served by the agency and using the right person to make initial contact. Accounting firms and other suppliers may know little about people with disabilities and believe that their capabilities are limited. Inviting these suppliers to organization events and encouraging them to get to know what they agency does may break down these barriers. This needs to happen before they are contacted as potential resources for employment or connections to other employers.

Asking an employment specialist to call the accounting agency out of the blue to seek an information interview may also yield limited results. Instead, asking the person at the agency that already has an established relationship with that firm would be more effective. This may take several steps as the contact person would need to ask who in the accounting firm would be the best connection for the people with disabilities.

Using the organization's networks can yield an expanded array of organizations doing multiple types of work. By carefully cultivating these partners as resources for people served by the agency, employment specialists can make their work easier as these organizations are more likely to welcome program participants or provide them with advice. Organizational networks also can educate employees on what is required to find appropriate work for someone served by their agency. For

© Jo Anne Schneider 7/2016

instance, an IT firm might identify a number of different ways someone facile with a computer could find work that an employment specialist may not know about. Expanding information and contacts should be an ongoing part of staff development as well as finding individualized employment for people with disabilities.

In addition to the social capital inherent in an organization, organization staff and board also have social networks that could be activated for people served by the agency. The remainder of this chapter looks at these networks.

Board Social Capital

Agency boards come from a variety of sources, including people with expertise needed by the agencies (lawyers, financial experts, etc.), family members, and others with an interest in its work. The networks of board members are another resource for social capital for the agency which is often overlooked when it comes to finding jobs for individuals served. Since board members have a vested interest in agency success, they are a natural source of social capital.

Consider developing a social capital questionnaire for board members. This would include asking them what professional and personal networks they would be willing to use to help those served by the agency find jobs. Rather than ask for individuals, ask what skills or fields are available through the board member's network that they would be willing to use to facilitate developing a relationship for a person with a disability with a similar interest.

© Jo Anne Schneider 7/2016

As with suppliers, board members would be more willing to provide these connections the more they are directly involved with the agency's services and get to know individuals with disabilities affiliated with the agency. This may include creating a board orientation program that involves new board members in the activities of the organization for one day and encouraging them to continue interacting with agency programs on a regular basis.

Board members are also potential mentors for both people with disabilities served by the organization and employment development staff. If the organization finds, for example, that many individuals in the supported employment program want to work in offices, connecting employment development staff with various board members to learn what kinds of support staff or specialized skills or tasks are needed in those office environments can help staff reach out to other firms using the board member, agency or their own networks more effectively. These networks can explain the frequent problems that similar agencies face that could be solved through job carve outs or customized jobs for people with disabilities. Armed with this information, employment specialists are more likely to recognize similar issues at other organizations and can speak more effectively with potential employers about ways that hiring people with disabilities can improve the bottom line.

These board members can also provide cultural capital tips needed to get people into networks. Through serving as mentors, board members could help people with disabilities learn the culture of their work environment. This could also include group conversations with staff and people with disabilities interested in a particular field.

© Jo Anne Schneider 7/2016

Likewise, board member's workplaces might be the natural first choice for an informational interview for a person with a disability. Take for example, Aisha, a young woman on the autism spectrum with an amazing memory for details and dates. Interested in working with the legal system, her agency set her up with an interview with a board member who was a lawyer. This lawyer was nearing retirement, but after talking with her, referred her to a larger firm that handled a lot of class action lawsuits. Aisha was eventually hired as a legal researcher to help assemble sets of cases with similar characteristics for class action cases.

Staff Professional Networks

Staff professional networks are important both as a way to build skills and as a potential resource for more leads for the people served by the agency. In order to ensure that its staff provides the most effective service, an agency should encourage staff to join professional organizations and perhaps subsidize membership. Staff should be encouraged to participate in training and enrichment events, not simply to learn their jobs better, but develop networks with other professionals. These networks can provide a wealth of information and connections useful on the job.

This kind of professional network can be formalized by a group of agencies or their staff. Often, staff with particular jobs meet on a regular basis, for example agency managers or employment specialists. These networking sessions are venues to develop relationships that can lead to swapping job leads that can't be filled by a particular agency or problem solving on finding work for an individual with an interest outside the agency staff's areas of expertise.

© **Jo Anne Schneider 7/2016**

Other networking opportunities come from professional affiliations. Attending conferences, keeping in touch with their college or graduate school program, or participating in online forums can develop these connections. The more connected an employment specialist or job developer is to professional organizations in their field, the more likely they are to provide state of the art services and remain in their job.

Professional networks also extend beyond people doing the same job. Staff may develop important connections to people in complementary positions – for example a housing specialist or staff working in educational organizations, that could prove important to finding and maintaining employment for people they work with. For example, if an employment specialist was working with an individual who wants to be an interior decorator, staff at a housing agency might know decorating firms that work in a furnished apartment building affiliated with their agency. Say an employer is identified that is not near public transit. A colleague at an agency that provides travel training might offer solutions.

Staff can access social capital related to their organizations in several ways. This includes the connections the organization has developed over time as well as that of its staff and board. These connections include both other organizations the agency works with in order to achieve its goals and its suppliers, vendors, and funders. Agency social capital needs to be used strategically, understanding that these are reciprocal relationships and that each person with a disability that a connection is asked to help reflects on the agency s/he is affiliated with. As such, staff need to ensure that both the front line staff using organization contacts and the people with disabilities served understand the cultural capital of those they are asking for resources.

Agencies should develop policies that outline strategies to engage agency social capital. That includes identifying staff with connections to various networks like vendors, board members, etc. and figuring out who should make the first call to such contacts. Another strategy involves creating a database of connections affiliated with the agency as a whole, its staff, and board with designated agency contacts identified in the database.

By leveraging the social capital of the agency, staff can identify a wealth of contacts that could aid in their effort to find jobs for the people they serve. Encouraging staff to use these resources and creating policies and procedures to do so ensures that the reciprocal, trust based relationships of the agency will be safeguarded and strengthened. Expanding both social and cultural capital of the agency and its staff benefits everyone affiliated with the organization.

© **Jo Anne Schneider 7/2016**

Staff Personal Networks

In addition to social capital related to the agency or their job, staff also bring a wealth of social capital to their workplaces in the form of their personal social capital. As with Marjorie contacting her friend Jane to help Caroline find the day care job, personal social networks can be an important resource in finding work for the people the agency serves.

Agency connections tend to be in silos – staff know people who work in their field or do similar kinds of work. Personal networks can often bridge those silos. For example, while running a welfare to work program, I built a network of nonprofits that provided internships for the people in the program. While some of these host sites came from other organizations with relationships with my agency, about half came from the personal social networks of myself and others working at the agency. We reached out to people in our faith communities, friends, and other organizations we had worked with over time as volunteers or just members of the community. That led to a much broader range of workplaces. Because of already established trusting relationships with other staff at these agencies, we were able to carefully develop appropriate internships for each individual and address problems when they arose.

When identifying potential mentors, resources to learn about a field, or workplaces, staff should be encouraged to reach out to their personal networks. This involves not just asking their friends, family and others they know well about employment but using them for advice on clubs, service organizations, professional organization and other venues to learn about a field

© Jo Anne Schneider 7/2016

and develop connections. Personal networks can also be a resource to learn about appropriate cultural capital for the job.

If appropriate, personal connections can be shared across staff. For example, many agencies have regular staff meetings where staff bring up individual cases they are finding challenging. Asking if anyone has a network connection affiliation with that resource can be part of these meetings. In this case, it may be best for the person with the connection to make the first contact with their friend or family member and ask if they are willing to help.

The tricky part of using personal network connections is confidentiality. Before reaching out to someone outside of the agency, staff may need to get permission to share certain facts about the individual they are trying to place from that individual or their guardians if they are under guardianship. Aspects of medical history or behavioral issues should only be shared when necessary. Stress the gifts and interests of the person with a disability. When reaching out to personal networks, staff need to ask their friends and family not to share details with anyone else not directly affiliated with the potential workplace. The need for confidentiality should be reinforced as these connections are developed.

Personal networks are an important resource for staff seeking work for individuals with disabilities. They should be used as a resource both for individual placements and as a source of advice on particular fields or jobs. Maintaining confidentiality is an important issue when relying on these contacts.

© **Jo Anne Schneider 7/2016**

Empowering Individuals with Disabilities to Build Social Capital

One of the most important roles staff can play for the people with disabilities they work with is to empower them toward independence. This is true with social capital development as well as anything else. Staff need to recognize the person with disabilities' already existing ability to create connections and encourage them to reach out on their own to foster resource rich social networks.

Start when developing the list of the individual's existing connections. Recognize that the individual has made friends or contacts through family, friends, faith communities, sports clubs or simply by being a regular shopper in a store related to his/her interests. Explain that these people can help the individual with a disability learn about possible jobs or fields and perhaps even help find work. Encourage the person to contact those people him or herself, perhaps doing role playing or developing an introductory script to talk about developing work related networks. Then ask the person to make contact and report back on what happens.

Fear of rejection or remembered bad experiences can serve as barriers to achieving this goal. If the person with a disability or family members claim that s/he can't make contacts on their own due to previous poor results or fears, recognize that this happens but remind the person that most people are kind and interested in sharing what they know. Perhaps role play the bad experience or ask the person to talk it through to try to figure out what went wrong. Then use this negative experience to model good ways to make contact or ask for advice. Remind

© Jo Anne Schneider 7/2016

them that nothing is gained if they do not reach out, but moving forward can yield more positive results.

It is also important to have realistic expectations of what a contact could potentially do. In most cases, the person may share some knowledge, tips, and other contacts but will have no tangible work to offer. Remind the person and their supportive networks that the goal is to expand networks, not expect that networking will automatically lead to a job. Keeping expectations manageable will lead to better results.

Once the person has used their existing contacts to start networking, encourage them to follow through on their own with new contacts. These could be with contacts identified through personal networks or ones found by the agency staff. Go with the person for the first meeting, then ask them to go themselves next time. Once the person gains the confidence and develops the social skills to manage these meetings on their own, encourage them to set meetings up and go by themselves.

After the person becomes comfortable meeting with new contacts themselves, encourage them to start developing their own new networks. This involves teaching them the key elements they should look for in identifying contacts: does the person have access to resources that could lead to work and are they willing to use them on your behalf? Have them make a list of potential contacts and talk about how to ask for a meeting. Encourage them to join clubs and groups and develop reciprocal relationships on their own. Ask them what they can contribute to these relationships and emphasize that they must be reciprocal, trust based connections if they are to turn into social capital.

© Jo Anne Schneider 7/2016

Empowering people to develop social capital means explaining to them how these networks can help and reinforcing the importance of cultural capital. Ask the person to identify the cultural cues that are important in that network and show how they can use them. Emphasize that these cultural elements are as important as connections.

Empowering people to develop social capital and cultural capital by themselves is a slow process that may involve many false starts. But it is essential to help the individual grow and become independent. It should be one of the goals of any job development process and is essential if a job is to become a career.

Building Social Capital to Help Consumers Develop Careers

Often, staff focus on finding people with disabilities first jobs, with some attention to maintaining employment but little thought about building a career. This is true of most employment systems for people without disabilities as well. How can staff help people with disabilities progress in their fields and gain skills necessary to advance?

One important strategy involves identifying mentors at the workplace and elsewhere. Note that the day care center that hired Caroline found an established employee willing to serve as her mentor to help her learn her job. Identifying co-worker buddies and checking that these connections develop into productive relationships is an important part of job coaching. Finding an older, established worker who can help an employee with a disability advance is equally important. These connections build both bridging and linking social capital for people with disabilities.

© Jo Anne Schneider 7/2016

While these linking social capital connections can be found on the job, sometimes it is helpful to ensure that the person has mentors from outside of the workplace as well. Mentors found through professional organizations, clubs, staff or board connections can both provide important advice and perspective on a first workplace, they can offer advice and connections to the next job as well.

Another important strategy involves ensuring that the person with a disability participates in professional associations or clubs affiliated with his or her interests. If the person is in an entry level job with no professional development supports, the agency may consider setting aside funds to pay for professional memberships or participating in conferences.

If the person is having trouble reconnecting to a profession, paying for professional memberships and conference fees may be important for job seekers as well. Take Selma, the HR trainer seeking work discussed earlier. Due to long term unemployment, she no longer attended conferences in her field or had access to the latest best practices published in journals. Paying for her memberships could provide the connections and latest cultural capital she needs to find another job.

This strategy can be used to connect people through informal clubs as well. Take Mark, the young man interested in birds. Participating in a local bird rescue society would put him in contact with people who could help him develop his interests, as well as professionals working in the field. The volunteer activities of the organization could provide both skill building and cultural capital, as well as important connections.

© Jo Anne Schneider 7/2016

Mentors, professional organizations, and clubs can also provide ways to develop credentials, particularly for people that may have barriers to formal training due to disabilities. If advancing in a profession requires formal training, mentors and other connections could provide suggestions of training programs with supports and tutoring to address disabilities. Or alternative certification strategies might exist.

For all these reasons, developing initial connections for people with disabilities should involve putting in place resources needed to advance on the job. This could involve a combination of identifying mentors and facilitating memberships in professional organizations or clubs. It could be as simple as offering subscriptions to journals or magazines affiliated with that interest that would include information on on-line forums or local clubs. In both cases, these resources build both social and cultural capital.

Building Appropriate Cultural Capital

The cultural cues important to access social capital are unique to that network and vary across fields, workplaces, racial, ethnic, class and religious groups, as well as across regions and even neighborhoods. For this reason generic classes on soft skills, workplace behavior, and how to dress for the workplace only go so far in helping people with disabilities find jobs and fit in at the workplace. Appropriate cultural capital is often learned over time through experience with a network and the people in it.

Disability services agencies and their staff can facilitate this process in a number of ways. The first important strategy is for agency staff to get to know the culture of key workplaces or fields where the individuals they serve work. This can be done by staff interviewing potential employers and visiting workplaces as part of their orientation to the job. While this kind of preparation is more difficult with customized jobs in many fields, staff can still learn what is important to local employers through active participation in the chamber of commerce, talking with local employers and paying careful attention to workplace culture whenever they enter a store, service agency or any workplace both while on the job and in their daily lives.

Caroline's experience with the day care represents an ideal situation because she already knew the culture of her new workplace through many years of participation in the camp. When searching for customized jobs, identifying these kinds of networks can be especially helpful. Ask individuals about their previous experience and if they developed an interest in working in a particular job from an earlier connection. Then follow up on that connection asking the individual to play an active role in communication as they will know the cultural cues better than the staff member.

Identifying clubs, internet based social networking sites, and professional associations is also an important way to develop cultural capital. Mary, Steve, and the other young adults with disabilities involved in high school and college clubs related to their interest developed social and cultural capital in this way. The same can be done for adults with clear interests.

Mentors or buddies that are part of the network affiliated with that interest or type of work are perhaps most effective in helping people develop appropriate cultural capital. Often, an individual with a clear interest like Mark and his birds, may have already made these connections. In other cases, when contacting clubs or professional associations, staff can

© Jo Anne Schneider 7/2016

specifically ask if anyone would be willing to serve as a guide or mentor for the person with a disability. Ask these experts in the field to share specifics of jargon, interaction style and other cultural attributes as well as information on the interest and potential employment. Using these mentors to develop appropriate resumes or introductory materials for job applications is also helpful as they will know what employers look for better than a generalized employment specialist.

It is also important to identify a friendly co-worker that will help a new employee learn the culture of the job. This is best done with the advice of the supervisor and explicit consent of the co-worker. As with Caroline, these buddies or mentors are important not just to learn the culture of the workplace but to progress on the job.

Social and cultural capital are usually built together, and it is important for staff to pay attention to both in efforts to leverage social capital to find jobs. Staff need to be keen observers when entering potential workplaces or talking with someone knowledgeable about a particular field. Information on cultural cues can then be passed on to individuals seeking work in that area as part of preparing them for the first workplace visit.

© **Jo Anne Schneider 7/2016**

Social Capital and Faith Communities

Churches, synagogues, temples, mosques, and other houses of worship are frequently mentioned as a resource for employment and social integration for people with disabilities. Faith communities are considered natural resources for social capital and the place where both social and cultural capital are formed. In many cases, these perceptions are true. However, not all faith communities build productive networks for their members or are interested in working with a disability agency to help people with disabilities find work.

The major reason that faith communities exist is to provide spiritual support and guidance to their members and others, they are not social service or employment agencies. The first mistake agencies make in approaching congregations is presuming that they will want to help in this way. Before contacting a faith community, do some research. Does the faith community host or support service organizations like a day care, head start, senior services or similar entities? Those already involved in this kind of service provision are more likely to consider a partnership with an agency around employment.

Most faith communities partner with nonprofits to provide social or human services, a small percentage do this kind of work themselves. Or they may rent space to organizations like a day care that is independent of the congregation. Asking a faith community leader if they would be willing to share their well established connections to the service agencies they work or volunteer in regularly may be the most productive way to leverage the social capital of the congregation.

© Jo Anne Schneider 7/2016

If the individual with a disability belongs to a faith community, it may make sense to reach out to that faith community to help identify networks to the kind of job they want. But as with any form of bonding social capital, be aware of the limits of that network. Also, ask how the faith community members perceive this individual. As with Kira and Mark, faith community members may have developed opinions on the person's abilities based on what they were like as a child, on the perceptions of a parent, or their own views on what a person with this kind of disability can do.

That said, in many cases faith communities offer a safe, friendly place to learn skills or find jobs. If it seems appropriate, these connections should be leveraged as a social capital resource during discovery and later phases of a job search. If the congregation hosts social programs and is willing, after a successful placement of someone already affiliated with that faith community, it may be appropriate to ask if they would be willing to provide connections or jobs for others served by the agency.

As with any other organization, agency staff will need to build social capital with the congregation. This may mean developing ongoing relationships with key staff and getting to know the structure of the congregation. Part of this involves understanding the culture of the congregation and that faith. Staff can not assume that all religions have similar values or work the same way as the faith communities that they are familiar with.

The Faith and Organizations project spent ten years researching the ways that social services, health services and education provided by faith communities were structured and the

© Jo Anne Schneider 7/2016

underlying values behind these programs. Part of this involved looking at the relationship between formal faith based organizations and their founding faith communities. These cultural capital differences are important for agency staff to understand when deciding to work with faith communities on employment related services. Readers interested in more detail will find resources at www.faithandorganizations.umd.edu.

Different religions structured faith based service differently and reached out to congregations for varying reasons and in different ways. Since even a secular agency wanting to partner with a faith community will be viewed through this lens of appropriate interaction, it is important to know the cultural capital that governs congregation participation before reaching out. Disability services agencies founded by faith communities may have an advantage. Even if they are now secular, these organizations may still have contacts in the faith community or with its social service organizations that provide important social capital. They may also need to evaluate their own culturally formed perceptions of connections to congregations before proceeding with outreach to faith communities.

The Faith and Organizations Project identified three ways that religions structure service. The study did not include Buddhists or Hindus, and readers will need to look elsewhere for information on these religions. The older religions formed before the enlightenment and Protestant revolution: Catholics, Jews, and Muslims, considered supporting those in need as a communal responsibility which they institutionalized through centralized structures. For Catholics and Jews in the U.S. this means that the faith community's response is centralized through the archdiocese and Federation. Synagogues, temples and parish churches may send agency staff to the social service

© Jo Anne Schneider 7/2016

entities created for this purpose if they request partnerships. Centralized offices may facilitate outreach to congregations and these may also be an important resource for agencies seeking partners. While the theology of Lutherans comes out of Protestantism, its structures are closer to Catholics with centralized provision of social welfare.

In Jewish and Muslim theology, people are obligated to provide for the welfare of others through Zakat (Islam) or Tzadekah (Judaism), concepts that are related more to creating righteous justice to lift up those in need than the Christian concept of charity. Learning about these concepts would be important before approaching congregations in these religions.

Faiths arising from the Protestant revolution - Mainline Protestants, Evangelicals, and Peace churches, on the other hand, are decentralized with the congregation as the major entity. Contacting churches directly would be appropriate in these religions. Faith is conceived as developed in the individual and providing for others comes out of individual calls to service. As such, the sense of communal obligation seen in older religions may not exist. Partnering with an organization may be the decision of the pastor or a committee, based on the beliefs of those individuals.

A third way of organizing service involves networks of individuals connected to a cause that are not grounded in congregations. Instead, networks are based on interest in the ministry of a particular individual or a cause. These networks may be connected by social media or participation in a specific ministry like feeding the homeless or providing supports to people with disabilities. The interfaith services for people with developmental disabilities come out of these kind of networks.

© Jo Anne Schneider 7/2016

In many ways, they may be the way in to other social capital connections for people with disabilities.

Recognizing these differences in ways to organize service projects and theology behind providing supports is important to any agency that wants to partner with faith communities. It is equally important for individual staff that want to use congregations to find work for an individual with a disability they serve or exploit faith based social capital from the individual or their own social capital. Learn about the structures and beliefs of the faith community before asking for help. Don't assume that they will be eager to provide connections or more complex services like hosting someone for a job. Understand that this may be a step by step process of developing social capital before yielding results.

© **Jo Anne Schneider 7/2016**

Tips for Effectively Using Social Capital in Employment for People with Disabilities

This section summarizes some key strategies to help staff use social capital effectively to help people with disabilities find work.

- Social capital means *the social relationships and patterns of reciprocal, enforceable trust that enable people and institutions to gain access to resources like social services, jobs, or government contracts.* People in a network look for appropriate cultural capital when deciding whether or not they want to share their resources. Successfully using social capital involves identifying three ingredients: connections, reciprocal trust, and cultural capital. Staff should ask these questions when identifying useful connections:

    1. Does anyone in the individual's personal networks, my networks, or networks affiliated with the agency either work in the field where s/he has an interest or work in a place that is related to that interest?
    2. Does that person have useful connections to places or people that could lead to a paying job related to that interest?
    3. Is that person willing to use those connections to help the person with a disability find work in that field?

- Social capital networks useful to help individuals find work can be found in the personal networks of the person with disabilities, both professional and personal networks of staff, board member networks, and networks that the organization has developed itself over time. Staff should be

© Jo Anne Schneider 7/2016

prepared to seek appropriate connections through all of these sources.

- Helping people learn appropriate cultural capital for a field or workplace is equally important if they are going to effectively use social capital connections and succeed at a job. Cultural capital is specific to a particular kind of work or workplace and staff need to be careful to recognize cultural cues relevant for a target type of work or employer. Some strategies to achieve this include:
    - Asking the person serving as the social capital link to a job to help develop resumes or job presentation materials for someone seeking a job in that field.
    - Asking the social capital link or a mentor to help the person learn the culture of the workplace or field.
    - Paying attention to the ways that people dress and act when visiting employers and sharing this with people interested in working in that workplace.
    - Encouraging people with disabilities to identify and participate in clubs, online forums, or professional associations affiliated with their interests and asking them to pay attention to the language, dress and other aspects of the culture of that field.

- Bonding, Bridging, and Linking social capital are equally important and should be identified and built for both individuals with disabilities and staff.
    - Bonding networks include people most familiar with the person with the disability, but it is important to determine if they have the resources needed to find work in the targeted field.
    - Bridging networks may exist through the individual's bonding networks or those of staff or the

organization. Look for bridging individuals or clubs or online forums that can facilitate building bridging connections. Remember that bridging connections also rely on enforceable trust and will not be created by sending someone to a career fair or someone met at a meeting.
- Linking social capital involves individuals or organizations with a reciprocal relationship that is unequal. Agency staff can exploit their connections to funders, government sponsors, or larger organizations to help finding bridging or linking resources for the people they serve. Identifying linking social capital in a person with disability's networks or creating linking resources through mentors.

- Mentors are an important resource, but the mentor needs to have access to resources that can help the person with a disability find a job and be willing to share those connections. Mentors are also a key resource to learn appropriate cultural capital and should be asked specifically to facilitate learning the culture of the workplace and field.

- Clubs, online forums, post-secondary education courses, and professional organizations can serve as places where people with disabilities can develop bridging and linking social capital for jobs related to their interests. These groups can also be places to develop appropriate cultural capital. Staff should encourage participation in these types of groups and cover fees or dues if needed.

- Developing workplace buddies and mentors through relationships with co-workers is important both to succeed on the job and move up. Co-workers placed in buddy or mentor roles should be willing participants with the goal to help the person with a disability learn the workplace culture and develop connections.

- In working with connections who do not know the person with a disability well, staff need to be careful not to violate confidentiality or get permission to share information that is not ordinarily shared with someone outside of the agency or the person's plan team.

- Faith communities are an important resource for disability services organizations and can be sources for social capital. However, faith communities primary mission is not to provide services or find people jobs, and staff need to understand that this would be an ancillary service for most congregations. Contacts should be made carefully and pay attention to the structure of providing services in that religion and the culture of the faith and congregation. Faith communities should be asked what they are willing to do and how they think they can best help, using their responses for guidepost for asking for connections or employment opportunities through based on this information.

© Jo Anne Schneider 7/2016

Appendix: The Theory and Research Behind Social Capital

While social capital was popularized by Robert Putnam, the concept was developed much earlier and has been used in several ways. Three major scholars are generally credited with developing social capital: Robert Putnam (1995, 2000, Putnam and Feldstein 2003) in Political Science, James Coleman (1988) in Sociology, and Pierre Bourdieu (1984, 1986 and Bourdieu and Wacquant 1992) in Philosophy and Anthropology. Alejandro Portes (Portes 1998, Portes and Landolt 1996, Portes and Sensenbrenner 1993), an Economic Sociologist, has also played a significant role in developing Coleman and Bourdieu's concepts.

Scholars at the World Bank, particularly Woolcock and Narayan (World Bank 2001, Woolcock 1998, Woolcock and Narayan 2000), have also played a significant role in furthering the concept as it applies to development as well as developing the concept of linking social capital. Linking social capital has also been adopted as an important way to understand patron/client relationships in the U.S. and other parts of the developed world.

These key thinkers' works have evolved into two camps. Proponents of Putnam's version of social capital, known through the work of the Saguaro seminar, focus on the role of social capital in civic engagement and as a community wide indicator of civic health. Civic engagement refers to participation in activities meant to increase the public good like volunteering, contributing to the United Way, or voting. Putnam defines social capital as "social networks, norms of reciprocity, mutual assistance and trustworthiness" (Putnam and Feldstein 2003: 2). This approach is used by scholars interested in community wide

© Jo Anne Schneider 7/2016

civic engagement and social capital is seen as generated through fact to face interactions in organizations that foster trust in the community. Since Putnam's works have been popularized in the United States and elsewhere, he is often named as the source for social capital as a concept.

The strategies disability services agencies hope to use to increase employment for people with disabilities are more closely linked to the research of social scientists who study social capital and social networks. Social scientists interested in the role of social capital in opportunity, social equity, poverty and development draw on Coleman (1988), Bourdieu (1986) and Portes (1998) work to explore the role of trust based social networks and cultural capital in opportunity structures for various populations. This research draws on earlier social network theory for individuals (Stack 1974, Granovetter 1973 and 1985, Burt 1992).

Coleman looked at face to face trust based networks that supported schools. Carol Stack showed how poor families rely on the resources of their social networks, but that the limits of those networks can hold them back. Grannoveter showed the importance or bridging ties to get into new networks while Burt spent his career exploring how social capital shapes careers. Portes has looked at social capital for marginalized groups like immigrants, showing how the connections people form in this country and the culture of both their bonding groups of other immigrants and the community where they are resettled influence life chances.

French scholar Bourdieu was interested in how societies maintained differences between groups, particularly those of different classes. Social capital was one of three types of capital:

© **Jo Anne Schneider 7/2016**

social, economic and cultural capital. While all definitions of social capital acknowledge that norms or culture are central to functioning networks, Bourdieu showed the real importance of cultural capital in defining who could access resources of a particular network.

The differences between Putnam and this social science school stems as much from the different problems they explore as different understandings of theory. While Putnam and followers focus primarily on the role of social capital in promoting community wide civic health, Portes and others from the social sciences focus primarily on the impact of social capital for individuals or marginalized communities. The World Bank initiative focused on the role of social capital in alleviating poverty (World Bank 2001) has begun to develop a middle ground between these two approaches by focusing on both institutions involved in community wide development and the impact of social capital for individuals attempting to gain access to community wide resources.

The definitions used in this guide come primarily from the social science school, with acknowledgement of Putnam's later contributions in bridging social capital. Theoretically, I draw primarily on Portes and Bourdieu. Readers interested in more detailed discussion of social capital as a concept and its use here will find more detailed discussion in *Social Capital and Welfare Reform* (Schneider 2006) and *Organizational Social Capital and Nonprofits* (Schneider 2009).

© **Jo Anne Schneider 7/2016**

References

Bourdieu, Pierre. (1984) *Distinction*. Richard Nice (transl). Cambridge, MA: Harvard University Press.
---(1986) The Forms of Capital. In *Handbook of Theory and Research for the Sociology of Education.* John G. Richardson (editor). Richard Nice (Transl). New York: Greenwood Press.

Bourdieu, Pierre and Loic J.D. Wacquant (1992) *An Invitation to Reflexive* Sociology. Chicago: University of Chicago Press.

Burt, R (1992) *Structural Holes: The Social Structure of Competition.* Boston: Harvard University Press.

Coleman, James. (1988) Social Capital in the Creation of Human Capital. *American Journal of Sociology,* 94 Supplement: S95-S120.

Fernandez Kelly, Patricia (1995) Social and Cultural Capital in the Urban Ghetto: Implications for the Economic Sociology of Immigration. In *The Economic Sociology of Immigration: Essays on Networks, Ethnicity and Entrepreneurship.* Alejandro Portes, editor. New York: Russell Sage Foundation: 213-247.

Granovetter, Mark. (1973) The Strength of Weak Ties. *American Journal of Sociology,* 78 (6): 1360-1380.

--(1985). Economic Action and Social Structure: The Problem of Embededdedness. *American Journal of Sociology* 91 (3): 481-510.

Portes, Alejandro (1998) Social Capital: Its Origins and Applications in Modern Sociology. *Annual Review of Sociology*: 1-24.

© **Jo Anne Schneider 7/2016**

Portes, Alejandro and Patricia Landolt (1996) The Downside of Social Capital. *The American Prospect,* 26: 18-21.

Portes, Alejandro and Sensenbrenner, Julia. (1993) Embeddedness and Immigration: Notes on the Social Determinants of Economic Action. *American Journal of Sociology*, 98(6): 1320-1350.

Putnam, Robert.(1995) Bowling Alone: America's Declining Social Capital. *Journal of Democracy,* 6(1): 65-78.
--(2000) *Bowling Alone: The Collapse and Revival of American Community.* New York: Simon and Schuster.

Putnam, Robert and Lewis Feldstein (2003). *Better Together: Restoring the American Community.* New York: Simon and Schuster.

Schneider, Jo Anne (2006) *Social Capital and Welfare Reform.* New York: Columbia University Press.
--(2009). Organizational social capital and nonprofits. In M.E. Harris (Guest Editor), Nonprofits and voluntary action: Theories and concepts. *Nonprofit and Voluntary Sector Quarterly*, 38(4), 643-662.

Stack, Carol (1974) *All Our Kin: Strategies for Survival in a Black Community.* New York: Harper and Row.

Woolcock, Michael (1998) Social Capital and Economic Development: Toward a Theoretical Synthesis and Policy Framework. *Theory and Society* 22: 151-208.

Woolcock, Michael and Deepap Narayan (2000) Social Capital: Implications for Development Theory, Research and Policy. *World Bank Research Observer,* 15 (2): 225-249.

© Jo Anne Schneider 7/2016

World Bank (2001). *World development report 2000/2001: Attacking poverty.* New York: Oxford University Press.

© Jo Anne Schneider 7/2016

Related Publications

In this Series

Using Social Capital to Help Individuals with Disabilities get Jobs: A Guide for Individuals and Families

Other Key Publications by Jo Anne Schneider on Social Capital (see http://chrysaliscollaborations.com/publications-workshops-webinars/ for links)

Schneider, J.A. (2010). Social capital and social geography. Annie E. Casey Foundation. Baltimore: Annie E. Casey Foundation.

Schneider, J.A. (2009). Organizational social capital and nonprofits. In M.E. Harris (Guest Editor), Nonprofits and voluntary action: Theories and concepts. *Nonprofit and Voluntary Sector Quarterly*, 38(4), 643-662.

Schneider, J.A. (2007). Connections and disconnections between civic engagement and social capital in community based non-profits. Nonprofit and Voluntary Sector Quarterly, December 2007, volume 36(4), 572-597

Schneider, J.A. (2006). Small nonprofits and civil society: Civic engagement and social capital. In R.A. Cnaan, & C. Milofsky (Eds.), *Handbook of community movements and local organizations*. 74-88. New York: Springer.

Schneider, J.A. (2006). *Social capital and welfare reform: Organizations, congregations and communities*. New York: Columbia University Press.

© Jo Anne Schneider 7/2016

Schneider, J.A. (2005). Getting beyond the training vs. work experience debate: the role of labor markets, social capital, cultural capital, and community resources in long term poverty. In H. Hartmann (Guest Editor), Women, work and poverty: Women centered research in policy change. *Women, Politics, and Policy,* 27(3/4), 41-54.

Schneider, J.A. (2004). *The role of social capital in building healthy communities.* Baltimore, MD: Annie E. Casey Foundation.

Schneider, J.A. (2003). Small minority based non-profits in the information age: Examples from Kenosha, WI. Nonprofit Management and Leadership, 13(4), 383-399.

Schneider, J.A. (2002). Social capital and community supports for low income families: Examples from Pennsylvania and Wisconsin. Social Policy Journal. 1(1), 35-56.

Schneider, J.A. (2001). Kenosha Social Capital Project education report: Churches, non-profits and community. Indiana, PA: Indiana University of Pennsylvania.

Schneider, J.A. (2000). Pathways to opportunity: The role of race, social networks, institutions and neighborhood in career and educational paths for people on welfare. Human Organization, 59(1), 72-85.

© Jo Anne Schneider 7/2016

www.ingramcontent.com/pod-product-compliance
Lightning Source LLC
Chambersburg PA
CBHW070401190526
45169CB00003B/1060